LESSER GODS

Lesser Gods 15 West 36th Street, 8 FL, New York, NY 10018, an imprint of Overamstel Publishers, Inc.

A VULGAR DISPLAY OF PANTERA

A DISPLAY

VULGAR
OF
PANTERA

TABLE

CONTENTS

OF

INTRODUCTION	10
EARLY YEARS	12
ANSELMO'S INDUCTION	62
COWBOYS FROM HELL	108
VULGAR DISPLAY OF POWER	144
FAR BEYOND DRIVEN	218
THE GREAT SOUTHERN TRENDKILL	282
REINVENTING THE STEEL	338
PHOTO INDEX	369
TOUR INDEX	375

FOREWORD

They say a picture is worth a thousand words. Well, in this case, all I can say is the pictures you're about to see are worth a million!!

All of these images left an indelible mark on so many, including myself. Not only are they incredible shots, but they also tell a great story. If you're not familiar with PANTERA, you should go back and listen to the stamp that we made—all over the world—through our music and the lifestyle that we led. For me, these images hold so much substance. Within each, lies an emotion, a solitary moment of who we were at the time, both as individuals and as a band. In them I can see not only the struggles we endured, but also a celebration of Life itself!

A lot of these "pics," as we call them, center around our beloved Dimebag because, nine times out of ten, he was at the center of our story, laughing and enjoying life to its full. It didn't matter that so many places, backstage areas and otherwise, looked the same, he made each one feel new and different, always with a joke or prank that created our unique fellowship. We were four thoroughly individual people, striving toward one common goal: perfection at what we did and Insanity, all bundled into one!!

—REX BROWN—

INTRO

It was the spring of 1985. I walked into the *Fort Worth Star-Telegram* photo department for my 2:00-11:00pm shift and flipped through my assignments. Of the three to four I'd been given, it was the last and latest one that intrigued me the most.

I was to go to a rock concert at the Bronco Bowl, a 3,500-seat venue in Dallas, with music writer Roger Kaye, who would be covering a local band trying to break through on a national level. After developing a strong regional following through relentless club touring and the release of two, self-financed albums on their own Metal Magic label, Pantera seemed poised for breakthrough success. The assignment was simple: meet the members of the band backstage, get some fly-on-the-wall shots of them getting ready for the show, and then shoot them performing on stage.

I was no stranger to Pantera and their musical abilities. By chance I had seen them perform three years earlier, in November of 1982, when, in my final quarter at Ohio University (where I was pursuing a degree in photojournalism), I was invited to interview for a staff photographer's position at the *Star-Telegram*. During my tour of the newsroom, I ran into a features writer from *The News-Press* in Fort Myers, Florida, where I interned the summer of 1981. After some small talk, she invited me to join her for dinner that night. We ended up at the Aragon Danceland, a club in Fort Worth, where, she said, there was a really good band playing. What immediately struck me about Pantera that night was the quality of their showmanship and how tight they performed as a band. They were covering songs by KISS, Judas Priest, and Van Halen—and, to my ear, they were besting the original versions.

I had moved to Fort Worth in January of 1983, after taking the staff photographer position at the *Star-Telegram*. My love of hard rock and heavy metal, frequently led me to seek out and attend rock shows at various clubs around the city. Eventually, during the summer of that year, I stumbled into a club called the Roxz, where Pantera had been hired as the house band.

They played four sets a night—three filled with cover tunes and one set of their own original material. I wasn't until midway through that summer that it hit me: this was the same band I had seen on the evening of my job interview nearly a year earlier. As a live band, Pantera was TIGHT. They could improvise at the drop of a dime and they already seemed arena ready. Over the course of the next year and a half, I fell into the habit of going to see them perform at various clubs in the Metroplex, such as The Roxz, Savvy's, and Matleys. Then the *Star Telegram* assignment happened and, from that day forward, my life would become inextricably entwined with the lives of the members of Pantera: Darrell Abbott, Vinnie Paul Abbott, Rex Brown and, later, Phil Anselmo.

Before I started shooting the band backstage that night, I handed my business card to Jerry Abbott, the band's manager and Vinnie and Darrell's father. A few days after the article appeared in the newspaper, Jerry called to say that the band thought the photos from the shoot were the best ever taken of the group and he asked if I might come to photograph them at some future shows. I took him up on the offer and began photographing the band at various venues around the Dallas-Fort Worth area. I also traveled with them to a couple of out of town shows in Shreveport, LA, and Muenster, TX. The more time I spent hanging around the band, the closer we became and the more they let me into their inner circle. In the summer of 1985, they invited me to Pantego Sound (Jerry Abbott's studio, where they had recorded their first two albums) to do a band portrait shoot for their upcoming release, *I Am the Night*.

In October 1985, I visited London, England for the first time and pitched Pantera to some of the music magazines there. *Metal Forces*, a fanzine that had reviewed the band's first two albums, agreed to publish a cover story using my photos from the album shoot. This was the first cover I ever got and it was professionally satisfying that it was for a music magazine. I couldn't help but think back to my high school days, poring over the images in magazines like *Circus*, *Cream*, and *Rock Scene* and dreaming of one day photographing rock bands like the pros. It was an exciting time for all of us (I believe this also was the band's first magazine cover). We were reaching new heights in our respective professions and helping each other get there. The band was ecstatic about the cover and the article generated some much-deserved buzz and positive press in the UK, where metal and hard rock bands are taken more seriously.

1986 was my last year in Texas. Although my professional and personal relationship with the band was flourishing, my job at the paper was becoming stale and I was eager for a new challenge. In November, I took a job at the Tacoma, WA, *News Tribune* and relocated to the Seattle area. It was difficult leaving my friends, both at the newspaper and in Pantera, but it was necessary.

As Pantera continued to gig regionally, I flew back to Dallas every chance I got to hang out with the band or join them on a road trip. I had no idea then, that our journey together would span two decades, five albums, and three world tours.

—JOE GIRON—

1981
1987

EARLY YEARS

—JOE GIRON—

In the early years, Pantera's sound was more melodic. They had a Van Halen party-time vibe and a David Lee Roth-type vocalist in the form of Terry Glaze. Heavily influenced by the bands coming out of Los Angeles at the time, their look was all spandex and big hair.

Near the end of Glaze's tenure as lead singer, the band started throwing a few "heavier" songs into their final set of covers each night, including selections from Metallica, Metal Church, Accept, Armoured Saint, and Judas Priest. Glaze performed the songs, but he was more into the melodic music of bands like Loverboy and Honeymoon Suite.

Don't get me wrong, Dimebag, Vinnie, and Rex were also huge fans of bands like Van Halen, KISS, and Def Leppard, but their musical tastes were expanding as they were being influenced by the heavier sounds of the bands who were just starting to make an impact on the music scene.

FORT WORTH—TEXAS

1985

—JOE GIRON—

From the very beginning, Darrell, aka "Dimebag" was the joker of the group. He was fearless and down for anything. The other guys were all funny in their own way, but Dimebag just didn't give a crap about what anybody thought.

On Labor Day, 1985, Savvy's, a Fort Worth rock club, held a special promotion to support the Jerry Lewis MDA Telethon. Pantera had the day off and I met up with the band at the club for some drinks and a few laughs. A local waterbed store had set up a bed in the club to raffle off for the Telethon. Of course, when Dime saw the bed his impulse was to throw himself onto it.

I had taken a business/personal trip to New York City in 1985 to meet with a photo agency that was interested in representing my work and to visit a mentor who was now a staff photographer at *The New York Times*. My job at the newspaper had created opportunities for me to travel and see more of the world, but this was my first trip to the Big Apple. The city was exciting and overwhelming at the same time. I bought the Statue of Liberty souvenir for myself—just an impulse buy—but when Dimebag saw it, he had to wear it on that Labor Day weekend night [Photo Index 03]. I did eventually get it back and proudly displayed it in my apartment until I moved to Seattle/Tacoma.

1985 →

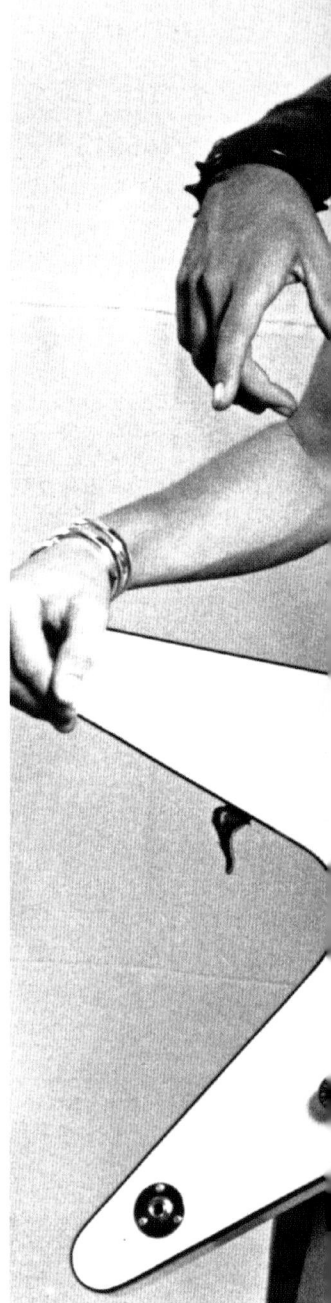

This photo is from the first portrait session I did with the band. The shoot was for promotional photos and album packaging for the *I Am the Night* album. I had done portrait work at the newspaper with solo artists, but I had never worked with a musical group before. I set up a backdrop and lights in the main recording room at Jerry Abbott's Pantego Sound, where Pantera had recorded the four independent albums and would later record *Cowboys From Hell* and *Vulgar Display of Power*.

Even in these early days, the band was utterly professional. They all instinctively knew how to pose in front of the camera. I didn't have to direct them at all during the shoot. They already knew how to be rock stars.

—JOE GIRON—

ARLINGTON–TEXAS

1985 ▸ FORT WORTH–TEXAS

—REX BROWN— Good ol' Joe!! We were down at the studio one day and our then manager, LD, told us that the *Fort Worth Star-Telegram* was gonna send out some photographer to shoot an upcoming show or two. We looked at each other and went "Cool" . . . Then we said "Oh, shit. Not another fifty-year-old journalist gal that doesn't know rock 'n' roll from country. BS!" The last thing we expected was a young dude like Joe, but the truth is, we barely even noticed.

When Joe came in, we were wild, crazy young bucks dedicated to what we were doing. We were solely focused on performing. We only saw what existed in the small circle we had created around ourselves, but Joe melded into that organically. His demeanor was so easy, so compatible with who we were, that he just fell into the inner circle. Soon he was showing up at shows all over Texas, taking photographs and documenting the life we were living. Sometimes he wasn't even getting paid. As we got better as a band, he got better as a photographer.

Meanwhile, we'd roll into shows with a hundred people behind us. He'd try to ride with us, but we wouldn't let him so he'd ride with a friend or a fan. But at the same time he was slowly becoming part of the team. We were a wrecking crew rolling down the highway, going from show to show. We got thrown out of just about every hotel we ever stayed in from El Paso to Baton Rouge. Dime and I always roomed together while Phil and Vinnie roomed together. Dime and I had a habit of forgetting our toothpaste. Joe was always prepared so we'd go over and ask to borrow some from him. At first he would dab just a little bit and then we started forgetting the toothpaste on purpose just to hear him say "no." It cracked us up. We didn't have a care in the world but it always bothered Joe and he made a decision that he would never give in on that. It's a running joke to this day.

We were twenty-one-year-old punks who could drink anyone under the table. After a while, we got Joe to join the party. Over time, he and I became really close friends, as he was with the rest of the band. I was street-smart and Joe was educated. But we were both well-read and that created a bond between us. You could say we're old souls. Vinnie and Dime were musicians through and through. School didn't mean much to them and neither did education of any kind. All they wanted to do was play and party. But Joe was close to them, too, and Phil as well. We were all different but we were all close friends and one thing was clear after a while: Joe had become the fifth member of the band.

Then he left Texas for a better job in Seattle and our big photographer was gone. He'd come back every three months or so to photograph some shows. As he changed we changed as well, from our style to our taste. He turned us on to a lot of stuff from his travels and we did the same for him. He was getting to photograph all these other bands and artists and meeting industry people along the way. Between 1985 and 1988 we got turned down by major labels twenty-eight different times, but he really helped getting us into certain labels and to keep things moving around us. He wasn't around like he'd been before, but he never stopped pitching us to any contacts he had and never stopped trying to help us get to the next level.

1985 ARLINGTON–TEXAS

—JOE GIRON— The Bronco Bowl show [bottom, far right] and the Six Flags Over Texas show [top left] were respectively the first and second Pantera shows that I photographed. From a technical standpoint, the lighting was great. The Bronco Bowl show had "arena" lighting and the Six Flags show was outdoors in the daylight. Before they signed their major label deal, most Pantera shows were at club venues where the available lighting was less than ideal. I've always preferred the ambience of "natural" or "available" light to set the mood. I loath using a flash and would only use it as a last resort.

1985 — DALLAS-TEXAS

41

1986 →

A spring 1986 show in Tyler, Texas, promoted by Guy Sykes (who would later become an integral part of Panera's road crew), was held in a large school gym. The band put on a professional, arena-ready show complete with pyrotechnics and Iron maiden-style stage lighting.

Terry would sometimes play rhythm guitar if the song called for it, which would beef up the sound even more, resulting in frequent disagreements as to how loud Terry's guitar should be in the overall mix.

—JOE GIRON—

Once Terry started going to college, we had to make a break. We had to find another way. We went through four or five different singers. We were just trying to keep our chops up. But we still had to play a bunch of covers. Then we met the one and only Phil Anselmo. Once he was on board, we got a lot heavier and that changed us for the better.

People were starting to come just to see us as a band so we could let go of the covers and start doing more of our own songs. That's when things really took off. We had a good fan base before but it doubled once Phil was in the band.

The club scene then was huge. People were buying the buildings next door to venues to expand the clubs. We were selling out and getting 2,000 people a night. Later, we had our own truck and our own lighting. We were putting everything into the band. The bar tab took whatever was left over. We did three sets a night. The contracts called for two sets of covers, but the middle set was just for us to do our own material.

—REX BROWN—

FORT WORTH–TEXAS

1987 →

I think the point when we realized Dime was going to be more than an average guitar player was when he was joining these guitar contests, at fourteen-fifteen years old, and he started winning. He was playing against guys in local bands that were twenty-four or twenty-five, and stuff like that. It got to the point where he won so many of them that they said, "Hey, you know what, you're not in them anymore, you're going to be the judge now." And from that point on, he had people wanting to endorse him—at an early age, before we even had a record deal.

—VINNIE PAUL ABBOTT—

DALLAS—TEXAS

1987
1989

ANSELMO'S INDUCTION

—JOE GIRON—

After moving to the Seattle-Tacoma area around Christmas of 1986, I would fly back to Dallas-Fort Worth as often as possible to watch Pantera perform and to hang with my friends. After Terry Glaze left the band, they had a succession of singers but none of them seemed right. Finally, on one of my visits back, I met the one person who could fit the bill.

I first met Philip Anselmo at the home of Carolyn Abbott, Dime and Vinnie's mom. He had just arrived from New Orleans and was being interviewed by the band to see if he was the right fit. This meant hanging out at the band's "HQ," having a couple of drinks, and shooting the shit.

Philip looked at me with curiosity, wondering who I was and why I was a part of the meeting. The band simply acknowledged, "He's okay," and nothing else was said about me being there. It was here at this meeting that I got to observe the first interaction between the band and their new lead singer. My first impression of Phil, was the he was a no-nonsense, intelligent individual, who commanded attention the moment he stepped into a room. He was also arguably the second funniest person I had ever met in my life next to Dime. On that day in 1987, a partnership was formed and a creative spark ignited that would elevate the band from a regional sensation to a world dominating rock machine.

1986 — FORT WORTH–TEXAS

—REX BROWN— Phil joined the band at eighteen years old. We had a New Year's Eve gig and he came in the day after Christmas. I picked him up at the airport in a friend's Corvette. We got to the house and the four of us got to know each other over a bottle of tequila and a joint. We'd been playing the circuit for three or four years and had a base of fans. He'd been in Razor White, a cover band in New Orleans, doing the same thing we'd been doing. We started playing all these songs we were familiar with and he knew them all. When he got in the band it changed the whole dynamic.

From the get-go he fit in perfectly. Our place had a spare bedroom and he stayed there from the day he arrived. Phil's a character. He's very smart, and, at the same time, set in his ways. He's the kind of guy who likes what he likes, and if you don't like it, he just doesn't care. He turned us on to all to all kinds of stuff we'd never heard before. We wanted to be an underground band with mainstream success, and we had a sense of how to do it on our own terms. It was a democracy. We were the perfect band for him to do what he wanted to do. And he was the perfect singer for us to be able to do what we wanted to do.

—JOE GIRON— My first portrait session of Pantera with Philip Anselmo as lead singer was done at Carolyn Abbott's living room in Arlington, Texas, in June of 1987. We taped some black plastic sheeting, the kind you would find at a hardware store, to the wall as a backdrop. For this photo shoot, the boys, who were beginning to shed the spandex and hairspray of their glam days, outfitted themselves in more denim and leather. This was the first time I had seen Phil since the day of his "interview" with the band and the first time I saw them all together "officially" as a band.

At the time, I happened to be in the Dallas/Fort Worth area on a sports assignment. The Tacoma Major Indoor Soccer League team was playing the Dallas team for the championship and four of the games were to be played in Dallas. I traveled back and forth between Tacoma and Dallas to photograph the games and, as luck would have it, I was in town at the same time the band was playing locally. They played that weekend at Savvy's in Fort Worth and it was the first time I saw Philip perform with the band.

1987 ARLINGTON–TEXAS   1987 FORT WORTH–TEXAS

1988 →

—JOE GIRON—

Vinnie Paul and Rex loved to go fishing. Vince had bought an old, rickety wooden boat, which he christened the "Death Boat." I accompanied them one time to Lake Arlington for a little fishing and a few beers. I took my camera along for the boat ride, but didn't end up taking many photos as I was far too preoccupied with the more pressing concern of my personal safety due to the questionable sea worthiness of the "Death Boat."

—REX BROWN—

For a brief time, Vinnie and I were avid fishermen. The thrill of catching a big mouth bass was almost as exciting as rock 'n' roll, if you can believe it. Back in the day, we used to drag another boat around all the time so we could relax after a week's worth of gigs. We had a trusted roadie named Kenny King who we made bait our lures and load the boat on and off the trailer.

Vinnie used to catch some fucking monsters. He just had that luck. I never could catch the big ones like Vinnie did, but I caught my share. It was always catch and release with us. We let everything go.

We called this boat "Noah's Ark" because it weighed more than a house and had more wood than the Ark. We also called it the "Death Boat." Soon after this photo was taken, the "Death Boat" went for its final run in Lake Arlington, Texas, and sunk to the very bottom by the dam, leaving us stranded with fishing poles and life jackets. I remember asking Vinnie, "Did you put the plug in?" He said, "I think so," as I saw it floating up in the water.

As the years went by, fishing was replaced by golf. I'd always been a golfer and Vinnie tagged along for about ten years. We played many golf tournaments together on our days off, hitting our way around the courses while drinking cases of beer and whisky.

 ARLINGTON–TEXAS

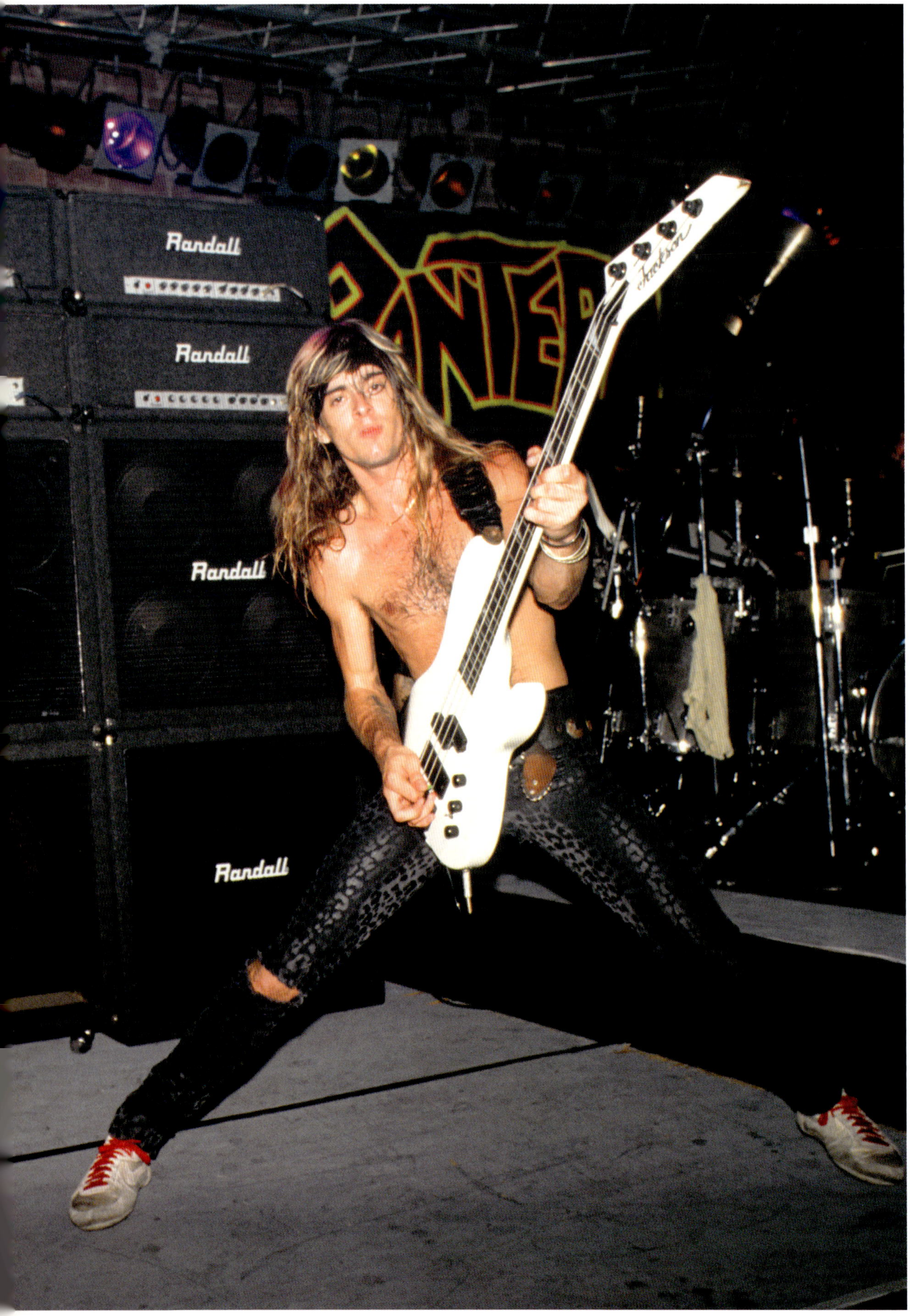
Randall
Randall
Randall
Randall

—JOE GIRON— The Arcadia Theater was an old movie theater turned music venue just northeast of downtown Dallas on Greenville Ave. The band rented the venue a couple of times and self-promoted their concerts, which allowed them the freedom to break away from cover tunes and perform a set of original songs. This performance, in October of 1987, showcased how ready Pantera was to conquer the world.

The best part of my working relationship with the band was the trust that developed between us. They readily encouraged me to get "up close and personal" while photographing them. Dimebag, who's creative process was inclusive and inspiring to everyone around him, in particular challenged me every day to take risks and to be as creative as possible. At one point, the band dubbed me the "the fifth member," partly because I was always around and partly because they had no issue sharing their stage with me so that I could indulge in my craft just as they were.

1988 — DALLAS–TEXAS

DALLAS—TEXAS

←1988

—VINNIE PAUL ABBOTT— Given the type of music we played, known as 'heavy metal,' Dimebag probably wouldn't get the kind of acclaim as Jimmy Hendrix or Eric Clapton, or some people like that, but to guitar players, he was the shit. And that's all that matters.

—JOE GIRON— Phil was an incredibly powerful front man who commanded the audience to pay attention to the carnage happening onstage.

—REX BROWN— Phil just had this charisma. It was bold and vulgar but he could be the biggest sweetheart in the world. As a showman, there was no one who could top him back in the day.

1988 — DALLAS–TEXAS

1989
1990

COWBOYS FROM HELL

—JOE GIRON—

In the spring of 1989, Pantera played a show at the Cat Club in New York City that would mark an extremely important moment for the band, as people on the East Coast were not necessarily familiar with this band from Texas. The venue was probably half full with a mix of fans and label A&R reps, who were there to check out this new band and see what they were all about. I remember that the band, the crew, and I had to stay in a hotel out near Newark Airport because the band could not afford New York City hotel prices.

In the fall of 1989, ATCO Records signed Pantera to a multi-album deal and the band finally realized their dream of being signed to a "major" label. At the same time, I was busy establishing myself in San Francisco and building my freelance career.

I didn't attend any of the recording sessions in Texas for *Cowboys From Hell*, as I was kept busy shooting assignments around the country for *Kerrang!*, a UK-based magazine devoted to rock music. I did, however, make it to Stamford, Connecticut, in the spring of 1990, where the band was mixing the album with Seattle producer Terry Date at Carriage House Studios.

I spent two weeks on the East Coast with the band, shooting portraits and hanging out. These photo sessions were being done in anticipation that, as word spread of this brash, fresh, new band in the coming months, music magazines would inevitably want photos of them. The band also played three shows at the Cat Club, L'Amour, and the Limelight in New York City to provide some much-needed exposure in this part of the country. The record label and band management were hoping to create an early buzz in anticipation of the album's release in July of 1990.

I shot the show at the Cat Club on March 21, 1990. After processing the rolls of film, I showed the slides to the band and their A&R man, Mark Ross. They loved what they saw and Ross asked if the record label could license the images for use on the internal artwork of the album packaging and on the face of the CD. Absolutely! Unfortunately, I did not get asked to photograph the band for the cover of the *Cowboys From Hell* album. The shoot was done by a New York City photographer hired by the label.

–JOE GIRON– Pantera had always been a "live" act; so the transition to being on a national tour was natural for the band. The road became their home away from home, and they developed a strong bond with their crew. There was truly a "Pantera family" and it was something special to be part of that inner circle. No matter where in the world I showed up to watch them perform, I was always welcomed into the fold.

The Pantera boys were well known for their prolific "drinking" habits. One night in particular stands out for me. During their first headline tour of the US for *Cowboys From Hell*, I had flown to Chicago, rented a car and headed to Terra Haute, Indiana, to photograph the band Warrant. I spent the night in Terra Haute and the following day drove back to Chicago, where the boys were playing a club called Chances R in Palatine. My plan was to hang out, watch the show, share some laughs and perhaps have a drink or two before heading to O'Hare to catch my 6am flight. All was going to plan, that is until the after-show party kicked in.

I remember being on the tour bus and Dimebag talking about this new drink they had discovered while touring Europe with Judas Priest: Jägermeister. Dime had not yet invented his signature drink the Black Tooth Grin (a large shot of Seagram's 7 or a large shot of Crown Royal, and a splash of cola), so at this point Jäger was the drink of the day. We had a couple of shots and I felt fine—or so I thought. The next thing I remember is waking up in my rental car, which was still parked in the lot at the club. The sun was up, it was 7am, and I had missed my flight home.

After an unknown number of Jäger shots, I had passed out on the tour bus. They had to get back on the road to the next city and their next engagement, so sometime during the night the band and crew had kindly deposited me in my rental car. Under the circumstances, they did the best they could to take care of me. Needless to say, I don't drink Jäger anymore. Whiskey, now that's a different matter altogether.

1990 NEW YORK–NEW YORK

1990 →

During a photo session at Carriage House Studios, Dimebag and I decided to get creative. There was a mirror on the wall and I shot his reflection, while lighting him with a red gel for effect. I shot other portraits of Dime, Rex, and the whole band in and around the building.

We also ventured away from the studio one afternoon to do a bunch of "location" portraits around the countryside. We found a nice cemetery during our travels, which I thought would fit in nicely with the song "Cemetery Gates," and took some shots there.

—JOE GIRON—

STAMFORD—CONNECTICUT

1990 STAMFORD–CONNECTICUT

1990 FRESNO–CALIFORNIA

—JOE GIRON— There were times when Dimebag and I would do photo shoots for his guitar and amplifier manufacturers. Around the same time the band was signed to their album deal, Dime started getting endorsement deals from companies that were recognizing how talented this young guitar player from Texas was. Dime was extremely loyal to Dean and Washburn guitars as well as Randall amplifiers.

1990 →

I next saw the boys in Dallas where they were shooting the video for their first single, "Cowboys From Hell." This was June of 1990, roughly one month before the release of their debut album. The "live" performance clip was shot at The Basement, a Dallas live music venue. It was the band's first experience with truly professional video production. It was a proud moment watching the band's hard-hitting, groove metal performance captured on film for the whole world to see.

In September of 1990, the band took a break from their first national tour to schmooze and perform at the Foundations Forum Rock Convention in Los Angeles. While in LA, they also shot a video for the second single off the album, "Cemetery Gates."

—JOE GIRON—

MARINA DEL REY–CALIFORNIA

1990 →

This is the year both the band and I were catapulted into the realm of international travel. The band would embark on their first-ever European tour, supporting Judas Priest on their *Painkiller* Tour, while I started the year by traveling to Rio de Janiero for the Rock in Rio Festival. Ironically, Priest also played the event and then would kick off the European tour with Pantera in tow in February.

It pained me to not be able to travel to Europe with the band and watch the guys experience new countries and new cultures, but at that point they were touring Europe on a tight budget. To save money they shared a bus with fellow opening act, Annihilator. Both bands and their crews rode on one bus. From what I heard from the Pantera boys, these "close quarters" eventually led to some fisticuffs between the two camps during the tour.

—JOE GIRON—

MARINA DEL REY-CALIFORNIA

1990 STAMFORD—CONNECTICUT

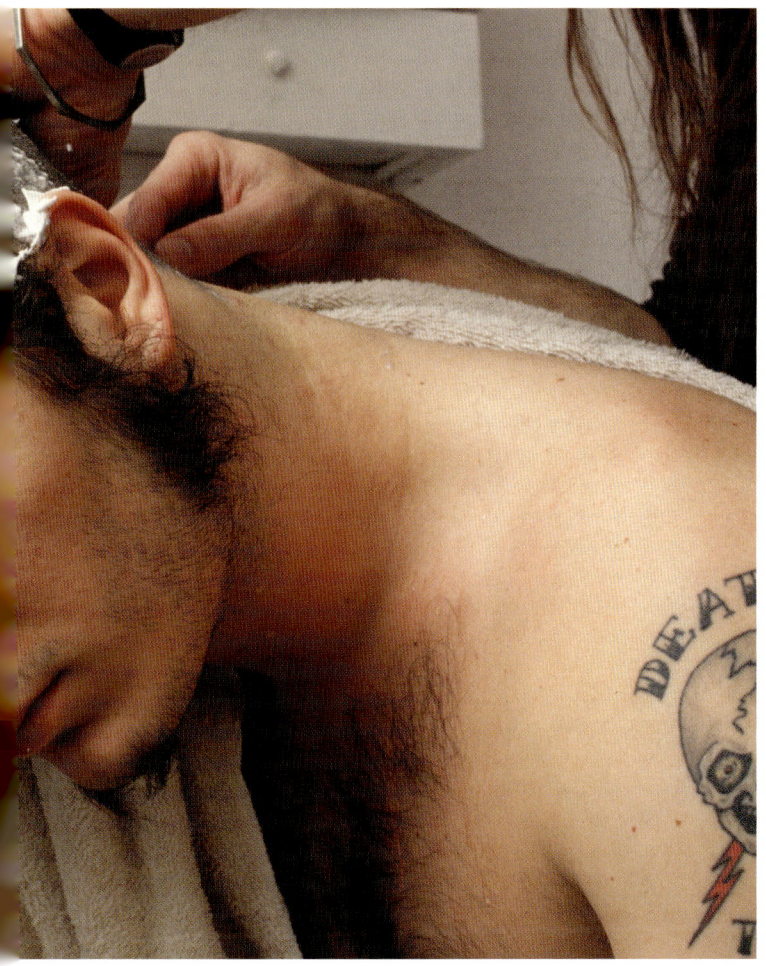

—JOE GIRON— Eventually Phil would have no choice but to cut off the braids and Mohawk. All the headbanging on stage was causing his hair to whip into his eyes, which was beginning to damage his cornea and other sensitive areas around his eyes. His eye doctor warned him he would go blind if he let that continue.

1991

1993

VULGAR DISPLAY OF POWER

—JOE GIRON—

If *Cowboys From Hell* was the opening salvo that announced to the world a hungry and powerful band from Texas was coming, *Vulgar Display of Power* was the album that took the band to the next level and proved they were poised for world domination. At the same time, my own career as a freelance photographer was really taking off and I was working with bands like Nirvana, Pearl Jam, Soundgarden, and Alice in Chains.

Vulgar Display of Power showcased how the band's songwriting had matured, while still retaining that underlying element of rawness that is at the core of their music. Songs like "Mouth for War," "Walk," "This Love" and "Fucking Hostile" would become crowd favorites. They were heavy, yet accessible in a way that is unique to Pantera. A new term was coined for the type of hard rock the band was playing: power groove. When I first heard some of the tracks at the Foundations Forum event in Los Angeles in October 1991, I was struck by how hook-laden the material was. I'm a sucker for a good riff and, boy, did these tracks deliver.

For me, the best part of the release of this album was that it meant I would be spending a good amount of time on the road with my friends in the band and crew as they embarked on their first headlining world tour.

1991 →

—JOE GIRON—

In early September 1991, I received a phone call from Pantera's manager, Walter O'Brien. He wanted to know if I was interested in traveling to Moscow, Russia with the band. They had been invited to play on a Monsters of Rock bill with AC/DC, Metallica, and The Black Crowes. It would be a significant milestone in their career, as well as a historic event, and they thought it wise to document the experience. I was hired as the band's official tour photographer.

Pantera was in the final stages of recording *Vulgar Display of Power*, and they felt this would be a great opportunity to take a break, clear their heads, and bring their music to a country that was just opening up to Western culture and rock music. Time Warner, Inc. sponsored the one-day concert and planned to release a documentary of the historic event. Mark Ross, the A&R person who had signed Pantera to their ATCO record deal, was put in charge of the project and once Ross found out that I would be there, he promptly hired me to photograph the whole concert and provide stills for the packaging, advertising, marketing, and press.

This was the beginning of a new chapter for the band, one in which they would become a worldwide success story. Moscow was just the first stop on the journey. They would go on to headline tours in Europe, South America, and Japan. I was fortunate enough to join them in Moscow, São Paulo, and Tokyo.

MOSCOW–RUSSIA

—JOE GIRON— Held at Tushino Airfield on the outskirts of Moscow, the free open-air concert was the first of its kind in Soviet history. There are no official numbers for the size of the crowd in attendance, but estimates range from between 500,000 to 1.6 million, with over 1,000 Russian soldiers on guard around the stage. Without a doubt, it was the biggest crowd I had ever seen and it would be the largest audience Pantera would play to in their career.

The band didn't have a proper dressing room, only a large tent to call home. The crew had to assemble equipment and tune guitars near some equipment trucks [Photo Index 16]. At one point, a group of Russian soldiers, mostly boys in their late teens and early twenties, gathered near the band's tent, awaiting their assignment. I convinced the guys to pose in front of the assembled troops. To this day, that is one of my favorite sessions with the band.

Even though they had been in the studio for the past few months, when Pantera hit the stage their raw energy electrified the air and they played with such intensity that it seemed as though they were in mid-tour form.

The only downside of the day was how the Russian police and soldiers treated the crowd. Never having had this much freedom of expression, the kids went crazy during the performances and the militia used heavy-handed tactics to suppress their antics. We saw kids being beaten, but unfortunately there wasn't anything we could do about it.

1991 — MOSCOW–RUSSIA

150

1991 → MOSCOW–RUSSIA

—JOE GIRON— Moscow was surreal. We arrived a few days before the show, which gave us a window to explore the city. We hit the usual tourist spots, Lenin's Tomb and Red Square, as well as the kiosk markets for which the city was famous. These were small, often illegally constructed, stalls where you could purchase just about anything—legit or black market—including vintage Soviet military clothing and gear, blue jeans, and bootlegged cassette tapes and albums.

We were told beforehand to bring cartons of cigarettes (even if we didn't smoke), as we could use them to barter with the locals and even to pay for cabs. We were all a bit concerned about what we could do in terms of alcohol, as we had no idea how much we could bring or how much we would be able to buy once in Moscow. Dimebag went as far as to fill an old mouthwash bottle with whisky, carefully taping the lid so it seemed as if the seal had not been broken. To his credit, he actually managed to get it through customs.

Everywhere we went, the band attracted attention. Some people knew who they were, others just stared in amusement. One of my favorite memories of this city was an encounter between Dimebag and a group of schoolchildren. Fascinated with Dimebag's pink beard, they gathered around him to get a closer look. Dime, who was basically just a big kid himself, was smiling warmly and talking to the children. He gave them some of the candy that he had stashed in his jacket and even showed a couple of them how to give a low ten, or "skin" as we used to say. His ease with the children and the kindness he showed them was inspiring. Dime was always wide-eyed in his approach to life. He was always looking to have the most fun possible. There wasn't a situation in which he couldn't find the humor. He used to carry a video camera around with him to document his experiences and people's reactions to his high jinks. This footage eventually became the basis for the band's infamous home videos, *Cowboys from Hell: The Videos*, *Vulgar Video*, and *3 Watch it Go*.

AC/DC
THE RAZORS EDGE
Pantera

SUMMER 1991

Date:	28 / 9 / 91
City:	Moscow
Venue:	Tushino Airfield
Promo Rep:	?
Sundown Time:	Who Knows?
Weather:	TBA
Dinner:	6:00 PM
Doors Open:	6:00 AM
PANTERA:	2:00 to 2:35
Set Change:	2:35 to 3:00
EST	3:00 to 3:35
Set Change:	3:35 to 4:00
Black Crowes	4:00 to 5:00
Set Change:	5:00 to 5:30
Metallica:	5:30 to 6:45
Set Changes:	6:45 to 7:30
AC/DC:	7:30 to 9:30
Curfew:	

Notes: Don't forget to turn in your Whiner Appication

1992 →

The Skid Row tour for which Pantera opened in 1992 was a pivotal moment in the band's career. It was a mutually beneficial arrangement, in which Pantera's heavier, hard rocking fans provided Skid Row with a bit more "street cred" and in return they were exposed to a more mainstream audience. They also developed a strong bond with the members of Skid Row and forged a relationship with their management company (McGhee Entertainment) that would serve them well in the years to come.

1993 would see both bands headlining their own tours in the US, Europe, and South America. I met up with Pantera in Amsterdam on January 30th of that year. They had just flown in from Denmark and had a couple of days off. The next day, the Dallas Cowboys, the band's home football team, would be playing the Buffalo Bills in Super Bowl XXVII and our hotel was hosting a Super Bowl viewing party in one of their ballrooms. That night, I went out to dinner with Dimebag and Tongs (the band's assistant and videographer), before joining up with the rest of the band and crew back at the Marriott to watch the game. The Cowboys were crushing the Bills and by the end of the game the mounting tension between the fans of each team had devolved into taunts being thrown back and forth. When somebody from the Bills' side threw a beer bottle at a Cowboys' fan, an old-fashioned barroom brawl was ignited. It looked like a saloon fight straight out of an old, black and white Western. Punches were thrown, chairs were smashed, and Tongs wound up with a broken arm. Cowboys from Hell, indeed.

It was tough for me to not be out on the road with the band all the time. Fortunately, I had magazine and record company shoots to fill my time and keep me occupied. I would not have been able to make a living as a rock photographer if I only worked with one band. I would drop in on the tours for a week or so at a time to shoot portraits and capture the band live. I loved traveling with the band to places they had never been and documenting the experiences they were having around the world.

—JOE GIRON—

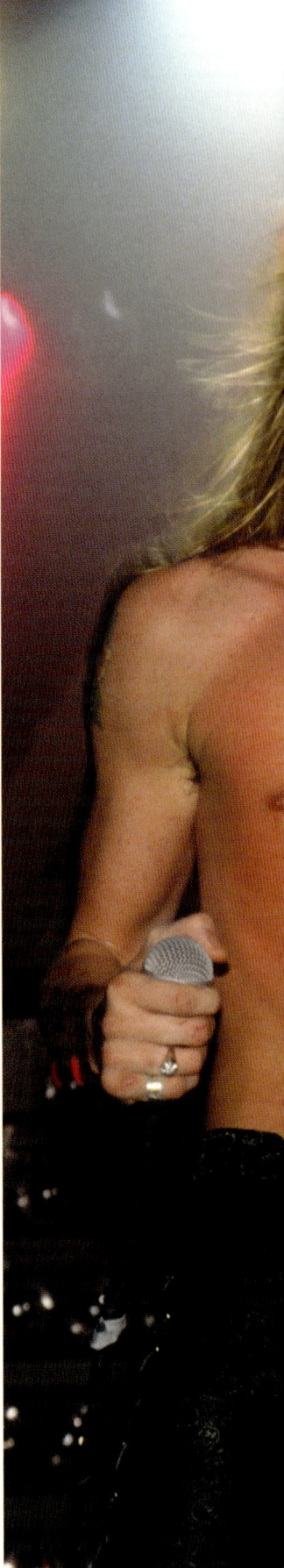

DOTHAN—ALABAMA

167

169

1992 → IRVINE-CALIFORNIA　　　1993 → SAO PAULO-BRAZIL

170

1992 ▶ IRVINE–CALIFORNIA

—JOE GIRON— February 1st, 1992, was Pantera's last date supporting Skid Row on the first leg of their tour, though they would return to support Skid Row later in the month after taking care of some promotional duties and headline shows to promote the release of *Vulgar Display of Power* on February 10, 1992.

The night got off to a strange start with a Christian group picketing the concert venue. Dimebag, always the happy prankster, could not resist this golden opportunity for a laugh. He got a kick out of provoking reactions from people. He had this small, portable amp that he often wore around his neck, so he could play his guitar out in public. He decided it would be hilarious to serenade the crowd of protesters with AC/DC's "Highway to Hell." The Christians were not impressed.

Pantera wanted to do something special to commemorate the night so they convinced Skid Row to jam with them to KISS's "Cold Gin" during the final part of the Skid's set. The song was a staple in Pantera's bar band days. To make the occasion even more momentous, the boys outfitted themselves in full KISS regalia. Dimebag decided to play bass so he could be "Gene." He fashioned a silver suit of armor out of Coors Light packaging and even concocted his own fake blood (out of a mixture of tomato juice and beer) to spit on stage. Rex was "Ace" and played guitar. Phil, who was the "Star Child" with signature red lips and star, dubbed himself "Bald Stanley." Vinnie, of course, was "Peter." Hilarity ensued and the crowd was treated to a truly unique performance. Moments like this cemented the bonds of friendship between the members of the two bands and forged relationships that have lasted to this day.

1991 — LOS ANGELES–CALIFORNIA

—JOE GIRON— Along the way, the band made many friends and gained the respect of their fellow musicians, who frequently came out to watch them perform or have a few drinks with them. This was never truer than when Pantera was in Los Angeles. Metal gods Rob Halford of Judas Priest and Gene Simmons of KISS, each made the trek out to see the boys perform and even took the stage to jam with them. Gene joined them onstage at one of the LA shows. Rob actually came out to Texas and jammed with the band at Joe's Garage. There was a great deal of mutual admiration between Rob Halford and Pantera. It was Halford who recognized their talent a few years before and asked them to open for Judas Priest on their *Painkiller* Tour.

Porn stars regularly came out to catch the band. They got to meet Ron Jeremy and Barbara Dare, titans of the industry back in that era.

In London, Brian May of Queen came out to see the band with his son, who was a huge Pantera fan.

1993 ← LONDON–ENGLAND   1994 ← LOS ANGELES–CALIFORNIA

1992 →

The thing that feels good is when I see him on video. It makes me feel like he's still here. He never turned a fan down. He knew that the minute he got off that bus, everyone expected the wild, crazy Dime that they saw in the videos and onstage. That's who they came out to see.

Dime always gave everybody everything he had. He stood out there, signing autographs, giving them guitar picks, giving them the shirt off his back—whatever it took to make them happy. That's how it was, man. He never came first—everyone else did. Somehow I know that we'll make it through this, and I'm going to do everything I can to ensure that Dime's legacy lives on.

He came to rock, and he rocked like no other. That's all there is to it.

—VINNIE PAUL ABBOTT—

LOS ANGELES—CALIFORNIA

—JOE GIRON— In July of 1992 the band made their first trek to Japan for a headlining tour. There were dates in Tokyo, Osaka, and Nagoya. Every show sold out and the fans were amazing. Traditionally, Japanese fans stay in their seats and show their appreciation by clapping, but Pantera's infectious "power" metal had the crowds on their feet at every show.

To liven up the backstage hours before the band hit the stage, we did a bunch of portrait sessions using Japanese props and signage.

We also discovered Kirin and Asahi beer on this trip. The best part was that they sold small "pony" kegs in vending machines on the street. Any time we ventured out of our hotel, we'd load up to bring back to our rooms. One night, we were riding back to our hotel in a cab when we spied a beer vending machine at an intersection and attempted to hop out of the cab. Our cabbie thought we were skipping out on the fare and freaked, but we somehow convinced him to pull over so we could stock up.

The Japanese thrash metal band Outrage opened for the tour. They introduced us to the sake bomb. For this deadly concoction you drop a shot of warm sake into a glass of beer and chug it down. These drinks made for some wild nights after each show.

A few dates into the tour, we met up with the Outrage guys for a late night meal. When we arrived they were already seated. A traditional Japanese table is low to the ground. You sit on the floor and it is customary to remove your shoes. The moment Dimebag walked into the restaurant, he made a beeline to where the members of Outrage were sitting and did a stage dive onto the table, shoes and all. It was highly amusing to watch the prim and proper hostesses chasing after Dime in horror at this egregious violation of Japanese tradition.

1992 ← TOKYO-JAPAN

1992 ▶ TOKYO–JAPAN

—JOE GIRON— Just three years earlier, Pantera had been a local band playing the club circuit, now they were embarking on their first world tour. They were well on their way to becoming "metal gods" in their own right with a devoted international following and I was fortunate to be with them at the moment they were making this transition. I had always assumed I would visit foreign lands as a photojournalist, but I never dreamed I would be traveling the world chronicling the exploits of a rock band on the rise.

The cool thing about this tour was that we traveled from city to city by bullet train, rather than on a cramped tour bus. This gave the band and crew the chance to connect more directly with the Japanese people. There would be crowds of fans gathered at every station and the boys would always stop to sign autographs and take photos with them.

The fans in Japan were hardcore, camping outside the band's hotel 24/7. This was the first time Pantera had experienced this level of devotion. And these fans were polite. There was none of the shoving or pushing to get closer to the band that they would encounter on future tours in other countries.

In Tokyo, we stayed at the Roppongi Prince Hotel, located in the heart the Roppongi district, famous for its active club scene and rich nightlife. The ultra modern hotel is built around in inner court with an open-air swimming pool at its center. July in Tokyo is quite hot and humid, so we decided to head down to the pool for a swim. Dimebag had heard that the Japanese frown upon tattoos, which at the time were still closely associated with the *yakuza* (Japanese mafia), and considered them unclean. We talked Dime into joining us for a swim, but he was convinced that they would have to drain the pool if they caught him in it.

舞台上手
Stage Left Wing

1993 →

I think that the uniqueness of our brotherhood was that we had a common goal. We never had to compete with each other. It was a magic chemistry that we had; we could just bleed off each other and it went back and forth, and it created some pretty tremendous music.

—VINNIE PAUL ABBOTT—

CLEVELAND—OHIO

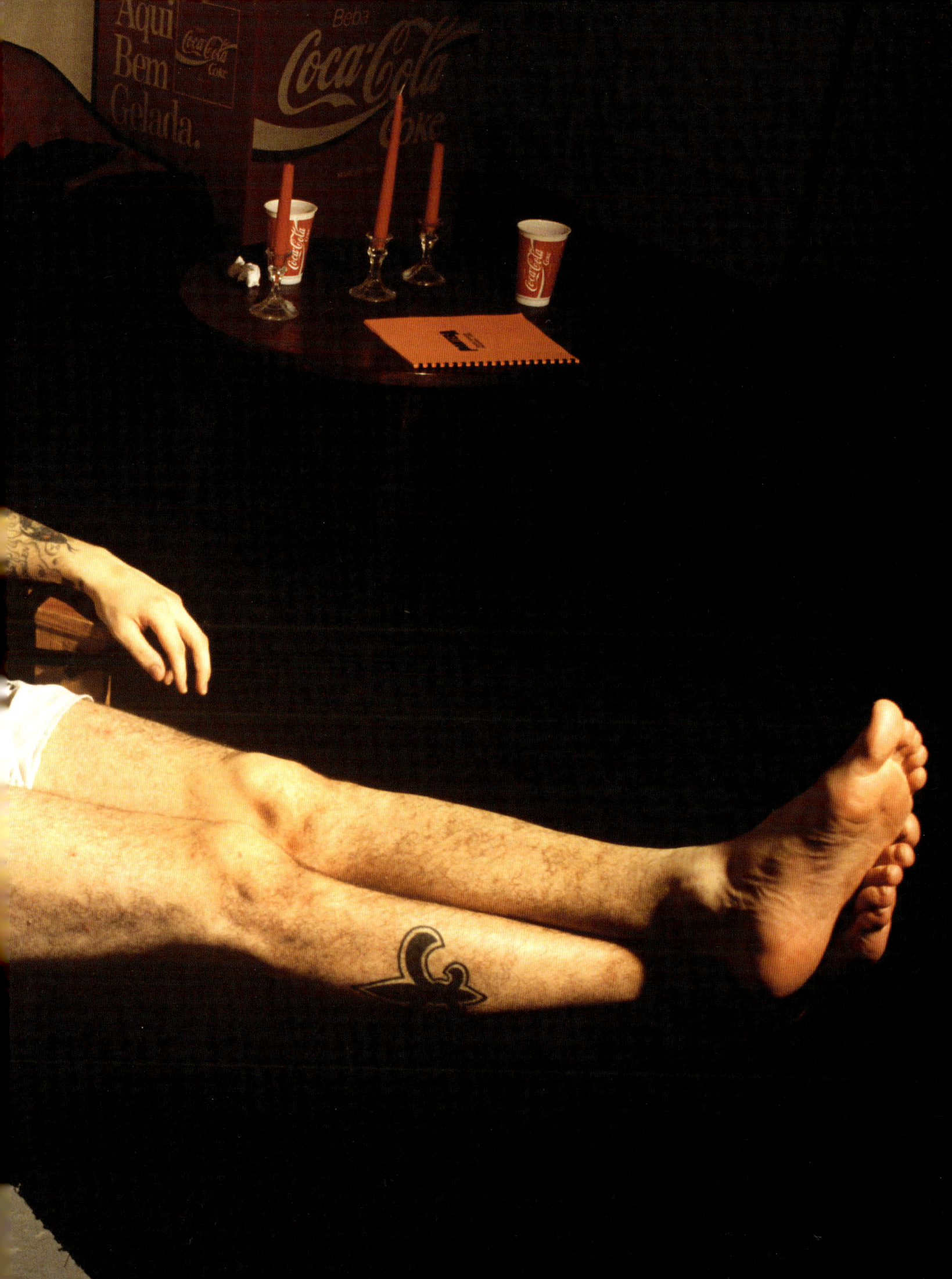

1993 →

Any metal band, or any form of metal band, will tell you Pantera was a heavy influence on them. Pantera was a machine. It was untouchable. It had the magic chemistry that so many bands try to find.

—VINNIE PAUL ABBOTT—

DAYTON-OHIO

1993
1996

FAR BEYOND DRIVEN

—JOE GIRON—

Never had a band as heavy as Pantera debuted an album at #1 on the *Billboard* 200 chart, but in March of 1994 that's exactly what they did. After the success of *Vulgar Display of Power*, while many of their contemporaries were moving in a gentler direction, the boys made the bold decision to follow up with a sound that was even heavier. *Far Beyond Driven* was raw. It was abrasive and heavy, which makes landing that number one spot an even greater accomplishment.

The band would follow up the release of the album with a radio and record store promotional tour before setting out on a world tour that would take them to Australia and New Zealand for the first time.

Once again, the new album provided me the opportunity to travel with the band. They were at the peak of their success and I tried to join them on the road every couple of months to photograph them for various magazines, and to continue documenting their career for my own personal archive.

1993 →

In the fall of 1993 Pantera traveled to Nashville, Tennessee, to record their third album. This was a departure for the band, as they had recorded all their previous albums in their hometown of Arlington, Texas.

Dime and Vinnie's dad, Jerry Abbott, had relocated to Nashville where he had set up a new recording studio. It was a welcome change for the band to work outside the comfort zone of their normal recording routine and the separation from all the usual distractions from friends and loved ones helped them focus on molding the songwriting for this new album.

Terry Date, who had been instrumental in helping shape the band's signature sound on their first two albums was once again at the helm. The members of Pantera are all headstrong individuals with a clear picture of how they wanted their songs to sound. Terry was there to help streamline the process and push the band to get the best out of their performances.

—JOE GIRON—

NASHVILLE—TENNESSEE

—JOE GIRON— Being in the studio wasn't all work for Pantera. There were plenty of pranks and an atmosphere of general "ball busting" for all involved. And Dimebag was always there with video camera on hand to capture the mayhem.

The band would usually eat a late lunch before starting the recording process in the late afternoon. Around midnight, they would be itching to get out for some cocktails and "tits" and, just as there had been in Dallas, Nashville had its share of a fine gentlemen's clubs to help the boys take the edge off and provide some end-of-the-night entertainment.

1993 — NASHVILLE–TENNESSEE

—VINNIE PAUL— I was over at Dime's house one time, and I walked into the bathroom. I came out and I said "Dude, you have a guitar in there, what's that about?" He goes, "Dude, that's where most of my kick-ass riffs come from. That's why my riffs are the shit, man."

That's one thing about Dime, he never ran out of ideas. He was never afraid to experiment. That's something that always blew my mind. A lot of magic came from that. He was never afraid to try other things; he was never afraid of people making fun of him. He wasn't afraid to fail.

—JOE GIRON— It was a privilege to be around the guys during this intense creative process in the studio. Not many people got to witness the evolution of their songwriting process and the intensity they put into crafting their music. When Dimebag would come up with a riff or a song idea, he would record it on these 4-track tapes. He had a box full of them. In the studio, Dime would start jamming on a riff and Vinnie Paul would add a drumline and then Rex would contribute his part. Phil would then get a copy made of the song they were working on and hide away somewhere to write his lyrics. It was collaborative process, in which every member of the band contributed to the creation of the music.

Longtime road crew stalwarts Grady "Grand Dragon" Champion (guitars) and Jon "The Kat" Brooks (drums) were on hand to provide support during the recording process.

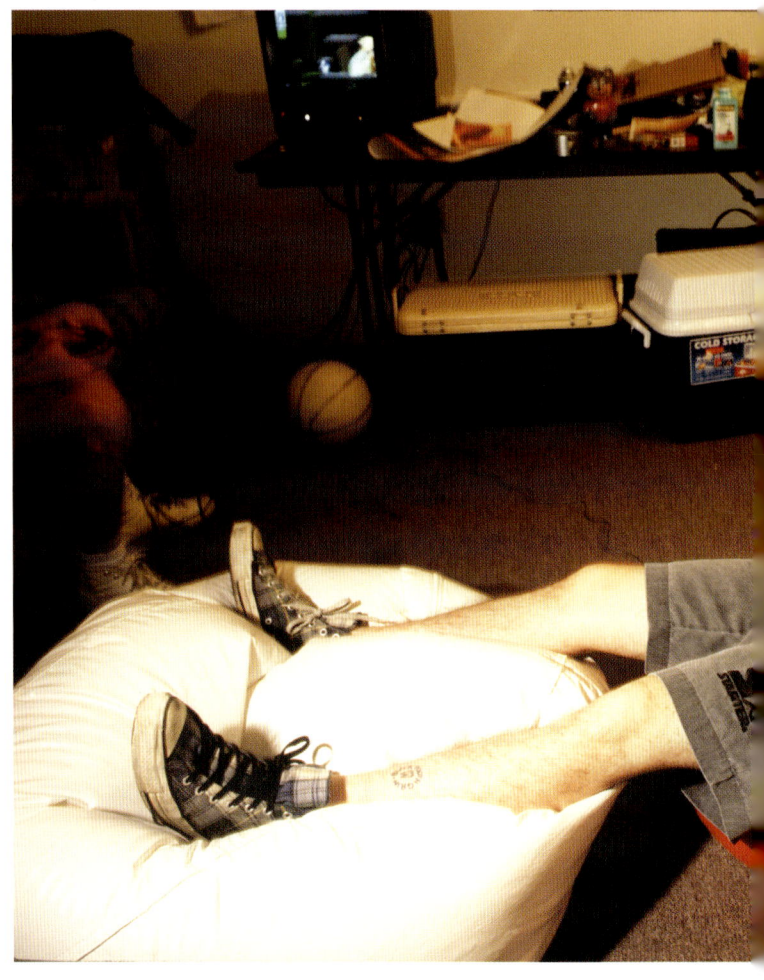

1993 NASHVILLE—TENNESSEE

1994

—JOE GIRON—

Far Beyond Driven would be released in March, but first Pantera had to master the album in New York City. I thought it would be a good idea to do a formal photo session with the band while they were there. The studio was in midtown Manhattan and gave us a nice, nighttime view of the Empire State Building from the rooftop. We shot a lot of set-ups, as I knew there would be a strong demand for new portraits of the band once the album was released. In order to give the images a different look, I experimented with cross processing (intentionally processing film in the wrong chemicals to create interesting and unpredictable color shifts and increased contrast) on some of the rolls of film from that session. It's a good thing I shot so many rolls that that evening. The band didn't like another photographer's official photo shoot done for the album back in December and the label was scrambling to find some strong images. I ended up licensing a few images from this shoot for the album packaging, as well as a bunch of images that I shot of the band while on tour with them in South America at the end of 1993.

—JOE GIRON— One night, after dinner, Dimebag and I ventured out in search of beer to bring back to our hotel rooms. We found a convenience store on 8th Avenue, a few blocks from the Paramount Hotel where we were staying. I had my camera with me and took some photos of Dimebag taking a few swigs of beer inside the store and then out on the street. He loved getting a reaction from people and figured he would see how far he could go with drinking out in public in the City. The term OG, or original gangster, was being popularized on MTV. Dime decided to have some fun with the word and parody the rap videos of the day. He pulled out a wad of cash and started "trash" talking while mugging for the camera. I was laughing so hard I could hardly push the shutter button.

Later that night, I took some personal photos of Dimebag in his room, chilling, having a few beers, and contemplating life. I shot some in black and white film to give the portraits a more documentary feel [Photo Index 27].

I rarely took photos of the band's private moments, only when they invited me to do so. I respected their privacy during "down" time after gigs, whether it was on the bus heading to a new town or in their hotel rooms, and didn't feel the need to constantly put my camera in their faces.

1994 ← NEW YORK–NEW YORK

1994 →

Pantera toured the summer and fall of 1994 in the US, Europe, and Japan before embarking on their first tour of Australia and New Zealand that November. As in other parts of the world where the band was touring for the first time, the fans were rabid and fanatical. Even when they were just doing an in-store appearance, the crowds were large and intense.

—JOE GIRON—

We'd always do in-stores to promote the record on our days off. We had a system down where we could run a thousand people through the store in an hour. We could sign one item from each fan, say hello, shake hands, and give 'em a beer so they didn't feel rushed. We just wanted to stay in touch with the people because we understood. We were normal dudes and fans ourselves. We had stood in line for KISS or Judas Priest, for example, just to get a glimpse.

—REX BROWN—

But it got to a point where we couldn't do that anymore. Ten thousand people would show up. It was insane. We were down in South America I remember, and the venue had a parking garage that was six or seven stories high and it was just packed with kids. It was like Beatlemania. We were standing there just trying to be nice to the fans, signing autographs, taking pictures, and our security was freaking out, like, "We gotta get outta here."

SYDNEY—AUSTRALIA

1994 → BRISBANE—AUSTRALIA   1994 → SYDNEY—AUSTRALIA

1994 BRISBANE—AUSTRALIA

—JOE GIRON— The tour was over two weeks long, which allowed for some days off and time to explore, see the sights, and hit the beach. We did some photo shoots around various iconic Australian landmarks. Tourists at the Sydney Opera House took interest in our shoot and stopped to watch the band with curiosity. At one point, a wedding party allowed us to takes some shots of them and the band with the Opera House in the background.

1994 ← GOLD COAST–AUSTRALIA

—JOE GIRON— The band toured New Zealand before heading to Australia. Dime and Vinnie took different flights with a few of the Dallas-based crew. They arrived in Auckland without issue. I arrived that same day and we had time to get settled in and even work out in the hotel gym before the others arrived.

Rex and Phil traveled separately with Big Val, the band's head of security, and Tre, Phil's assistant. They were to catch a connecting flight to Auckland at LAX, but it turned into a comedy of errors when that flight was delayed and they found themselves waiting it out at the nearest bar. By the time they boarded the plane, Phil and Rex had enjoyed more than a few adult beverages. Phil didn't like the way some of the other business class passengers were "eyeing" him. He made a scene and they were all kicked off the flight. In the chaos, Big Val left his fanny pack on the plane and by the time he realized it was missing the flight had departed.

There were no more flights to Auckland that day, so the unlucky traveling party spent the night at a local airport hotel and boarded a new flight the next day. Because of the incident on the plane the day before, their flight records had been flagged so when they arrived in New Zealand, they were treated to the "royal" Immigration and Customs entry screening—the kind that requires latex gloves, if you know what I mean. Because of this fiasco, the band lost a full day of pre-production, but fortunately for the tour it all worked out in the end.

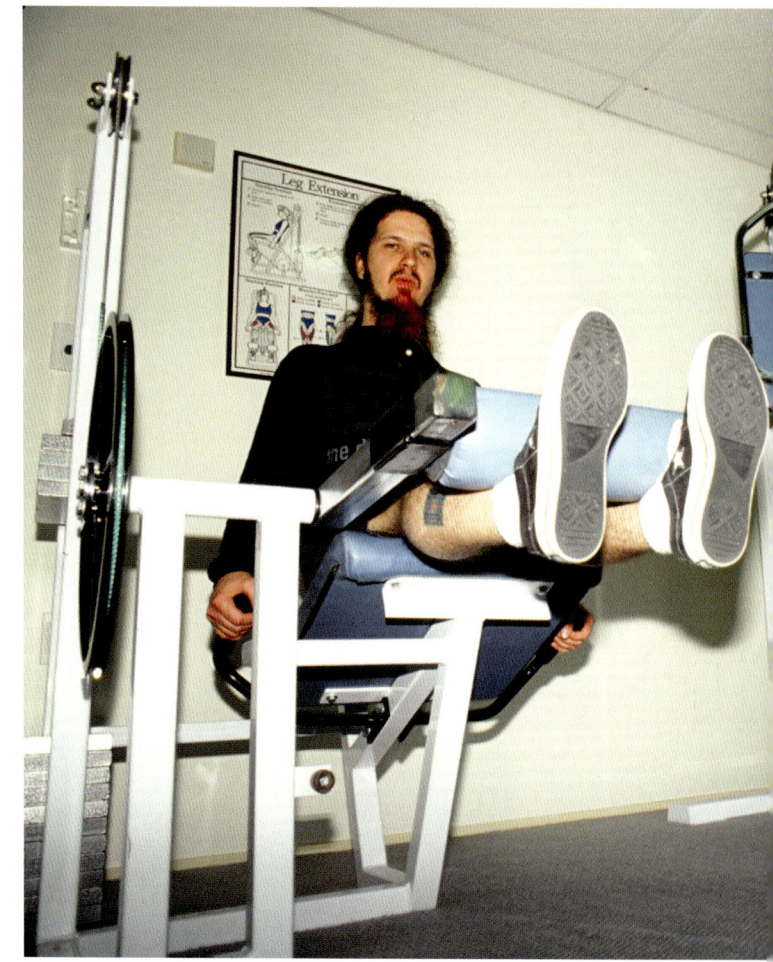

1994 AUCKLAND—NEW ZEALAND

1994 — SYDNEY–AUSTRALIA

—JOE GIRON— At in-store appearances, the band would stay as long as it took to greet every single one of their fans. They came armed with all kinds of things for the boys to sign: memorabilia, albums, CD's, posters, even their own skin. Whatever they wanted signed, the boys were happy to oblige. At one signing in Australia, a young wheelchair-bound fan was having a hard time getting close to the band. Some people waiting in line lifted him onto the table, so he could get pictures taken with them more easily. It was heartwarming to see Pantera fans helping one another out.

We partied hard, or "tore it up" as we liked to call it, throughout this tour. The good people of Australia and New Zealand did not fail to live up to their reputation as serious drinkers. There were times when making the shuttle call for the airport to catch the next flight was painful and difficult. We would grab sleep wherever possible, much to the chagrin of the general public in the boarding areas of the airport.

One time, while waiting for our delayed flight from Sydney to Melbourne, Dime decided it would be a good idea to do a shot of liquor. It was 11 o'clock in the morning. We had all indulged in some heavy post-show drinking, following the band's performance at the Sydney Entertainment Centre the night before. I tried to excuse myself from downing the shot, but Dime would have none of it. I got it down my neck, but just as soon as it went down it came right back up again (and into a planter, housing an unsuspecting fern). I caught some grief for that and, as a penalty, had to drink another shot. Thankfully, this one stayed down.

1994 AUCKLAND–NEW ZEALAND

249

1994 →

—JOE GIRON—

Over the course of my many years photographing the band, we did numerous photo shoots together. Although they didn't always want to, they never failed to put in the necessary hours for me to capture the images I needed, whether it was for packaging or publicity shots for the record label or cover images for high profile music magazines.

When the band was on the road, photo shoots usually happened at the venue, and almost always right before they hit the stage. It was incumbent upon me to find the right location, preferably one that wasn't too far from their dressing room, or better yet one that was on the way to the stage. Dime was always there to push my buttons to see how I would react during the shoots—like pouring beer right into my lens. My newspaper background helped to keep me calm in those moments.

—REX BROWN—

All of us were natural musicians. We played together so well that we instinctively knew where each was going to go. I've played with many people since then but there's never been that kind of magic. We were all bullheaded fucks but once you had us in the same room there was a chemistry between the four of us. I called it *magic in a box*. It has been copied and imitated time and time again, but NO ONE did it in the way the four guys you see here did!

UNIONDALE—NEW YORK

1995

—REX BROWN— Pantera fans have been with us since day one, from the night we were playing to eight people in Long Island, Maine, on our first national tour, to the time we started headlining international festivals and playing to close to a million people, if not more, in Moscow and beyond.

Far Beyond Driven was a result of that hard work and went to Number 1 in twenty-six countries. When we left Texas, it was album/tour, album/tour cycles for years. We never saw home. Our first tour was 338 days, then into the studio for five or six weeks and then back on the road for sixteen to seventeen months straight.

Pantera fans are the most dedicated, cult-like, diehard fans you could ever ask for. They live with Pantera still and we haven't made a lick of music in years. I guess it means we did our job right and left an indelible mark. I don't think we ever let our fans down in this roller coaster of life called rock 'n' roll, or in what we achieved as one of the baddest bands of our era and beyond!!

—JOE GIRON— Pantera continued to tour the US and finished up the final leg of the *Far Beyond Driven* Tour in Las Vegas, Nevada in April 1995, before heading to South America for shows in Brazil and Argentina. The final US show, at the Thomas & Mack Arena, was highlighted by opening band, Type O Negative, covering the Pantera stage with so much toilet paper that the Las Vegas Fire Marshall deemed it a fire hazard. The venue banned Pantera from playing there for a few years as a result of this prank.

1994 → CLEVELAND-OHIO   1995 → ORLANDO-FLORIDA

1994 ⟶ IRVINE–CALIFORNIA

—JOE GIRON— At the same time Pantera was touring *Far Beyond Driven*, Nine Inch Nails were on the road supporting *The Downward Spiral*. As the two bands crisscrossed the country they would often find themselves in the same city. This led to many a night off where either Pantera or NIN would come out see one another's show. Both camps hosted after-show parties backstage that were pretty out of hand [Photo Index 28]. The revelry was fueled by the designer drug ecstasy, which had become hugely popular at that time. It was pretty mind blowing seeing a NIN show after having taken a half or quarter hit of ecstasy.

1994 — UNIONDALE–NEW YORK

—JOE GIRON— Pantera's capacity for alcohol consumption was legendary, and the *Far Beyond Driven* Tour was no exception. The band decided to take it to the next level and share their booze with the crowd during the show. The road crew would line up plastic cups, filled with a small amount of beer, on the top of a road case that was then rolled out onto the stage. The band would toss the cups out to their fans, hoping the beer wouldn't spill. For the most part, the trick was surprisingly successful, but there were plenty of times when the fans got soaked—though, they didn't seem to mind. This tour ritual also had the added benefit of allowing the band to take a quick breather about three quarters of the way into their set and drink a shot or two of whiskey with each other.

1994 DAYTON–OHIO

271

1996
1997

THE GREAT SOUTHERN TRENDKILL

—JOE GIRON—

After the success of *Far Beyond Driven*, Pantera was riding high. Determined to steer clear of the pitfalls of some of their contemporaries, who were venturing down more "radio friendly" paths, Pantera decided to move in the exact opposite direction. Nu metal and grunge were all the rage and they wanted to set themselves apart from those genres as much as possible. The result was *The Great Southern Trendkill*, an album that was heavier, brasher, and moodier than anything they had done before. I had no idea that was even possible.

1996 →

Dimebag had a restless and creative mind. To alleviate the relentless boredom of being on the road, he would create characters that he could inhabit in order to draw a reaction from those around him, or just to "bust a nut"—Dime-bonics for "have a laugh." Dime-bonics was the term we used for Darrell's special language. He often invented his own words and phrases, and if you were not familiar you might have no idea what he was talking about.

One of these characters was the Local Yokel. Dimebag was proud of his Texas heritage and the Local Yokel was his homage to where he'd come from and some of the people he'd known growing up. I personally always thought he was also paying tribute to another, proud, Texas band: ZZ Top.

—JOE GIRON—

1996 — DALWORTHINGTON GARDENS–TEXAS

—JOE GIRON— We returned to Dallas to shoot the album packaging for *The Great Southern Trendkill*. Dimebag and I were hanging out at his house, when he came up with an idea to shoot some macabre, satanic portraits as a way of poking fun at the stereotypical perception of metal music as "the devil's music." Despite his demonic look in the portraits, we had a lot of laughs during this shoot.

Dimebag loved Taco Bell. It was his go-to "bus food" every night on tour. But when he discovered Del Taco on a trip to California that became his new favorite fast food Mexican joint anytime he was in the Golden State. He loved their "Del Scorcho" hot sauce and while mixing the album in Los Angeles, Dime bought several boxes of it.

While they were touring in Northern Carolina, we came up with the idea of trying to get a Del Taco sponsorship deal. We did a portrait shoot, featuring Del Scorcho prominently on one of his guitars. A friend of mine in the music industry with ties to some corporate clients made the pitch to the company and submitted my images. Unfortunately, however, Philip's overdose a couple of weeks later put the kibosh on that idea.

1996 — WINSTON-SALEM—NORTH CAROLINA

1996 →

In 1996, Washburn, Dimebag's guitar manufacturer, produced and marketed a line of signature guitars for him: Black Jack, Lightning Bolt, Rebel Flag, and Dime Slime. We did a series of portraits to use in advertisements to promote and sell the series. We shot in and around Arlington, Texas, choosing locations that complemented the specific design we were photographing.

For the Black Jack guitar, we shot at a local strip club that housed a Blackjack table and we found a local creek in the countryside that had a southern, swamp-like feel for the Rebel Flag.

We had the most fun shooting the Dime Slime guitar, which we did at Dime's house. We cut a hole in a kiddie pool and lined it with black plastic. We then cut a hole in the plastic and slid Dime into the two holes, and we covered him and the guitar with a homemade green, slimy papier-mâché concoction.

—JOE GIRON—

ARLINGTON—TEXAS

1997 → DENVER–COLORADO　　　1996 → ANTIOCH–TENNESSEE

1996 ANTIOCH—TENNESSEE

—JOE GIRON— June of 1996 saw the beginning of the touring cycle for *The Great Southern Trendkill* at the LJVM Coliseum in Winston Salem, NC. The bill featured both Pantera and White Zombie as co-headliners. This was the biggest tour Pantera had ever undertaken, requiring four 18-wheelers and six tour buses to transport the equipment, both bands, and their crews from venue to venue.

Concrete Management, which managed both bands at the time, had formulated the concept for the tour. White Zombie's show was theatrical, with backdrops, lighting, masks, and other props all over the stage. Since it was would be easier to set up their intensive stage set before the show, rather than load in and load out between the opening band and a headlining Pantera, it was decided that White Zombie would close the show on this set of dates.

It irked the Pantera camp that they had to take the stage before White Zombie and I thought it was a big mistake for Zombie to close. What band in their right mind would want to follow Pantera? No other band at the time that could match the musicianship, tightness, and brutality of Pantera live. My instinct proved correct. On some of the dates I came out to watch the show, they completely blew Zombie off the stage and many audience members left after Pantera's set.

1996 — BIRMINGHAM–ALABAMA

—JOE GIRON— Pantera fans would go to great lengths to get the band's attention, often by dressing up in crazy outfits. One of the most memorable for me was a guy in Birmingham, Alabama who showed up at photo shoot Dime and I were doing with his guitars and backline equipment at the Oak Mountain Amphitheater. He had on this zany homemade outfit, topped with an animal skull and antlers. Of course, Dime loved it and the costumed fan was soon incorporated into our shoot. It was so off the wall that I ended up bringing in the rest of the band for a special portrait.

Boredom while waiting to take the stage was the biggest obstacle for the band to overcome when they were on the road. Many of my solo portrait shoots with Dime were done simply to pass the time.

1997 ← DENVER–COLORADO   1996 ← BIRMINGHAM–ALABAMA

1996 — INGLEWOOD–CALIFORNIA

—JOE GIRON— Between sets of the show at the Oak Mountain Amphitheater, I did a portrait session with Pantera and White Zombie. The two bands got along extremely well and I knew that my magazine clients would gladly publish the images. Although Rob Zombie never really hung out and drank with Pantera, all the other members of the band gladly availed themselves of the party atmosphere that surrounded Pantera. To put it bluntly, it was pretty boring in the White Zombie dressing room.

Pantera welcomed opening bands into their world with open arms. It was a badge of honor to say you partied with Pantera and survived to tell the tale. I remember a press agent that worked for Pantera's UK record company telling me a story about his backstage experience with the band. He said the band made him drink so many Black Tooths that he had woken up in a field somewhere in the English countryside with no memory of how he got there.

1996 — TULSA–OKLAHOMA   1996 — BIRMINGHAM–ALABAMA

DALWORTHINGTON GARDENS–TEXAS

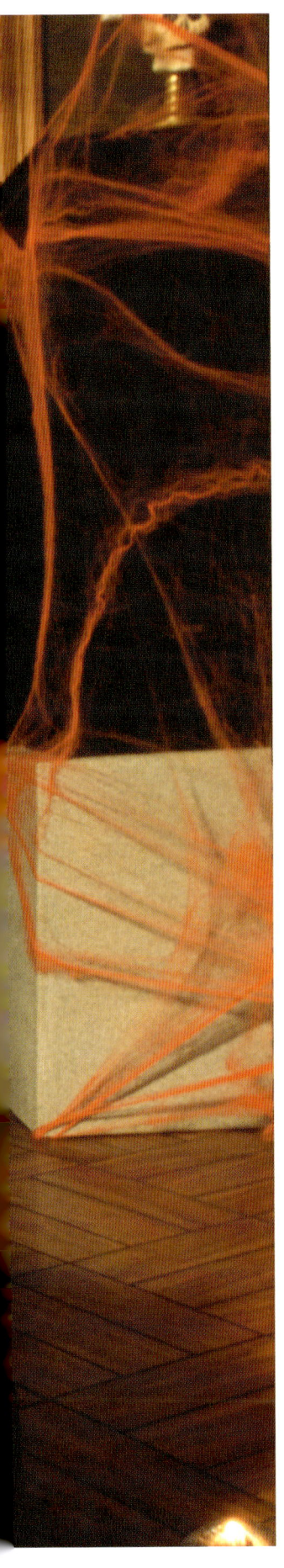

1996

—JOE GIRON— During a break from touring later that year, I was flown to Dallas to photograph Dimebag "at home" for a monthly feature in a British metal magazine. The premise was to capture rock musicians in the comfort of their own homes. We decided to class up the shoot with pics of Dime drinking Coors Light from a wine glass.

1996 — DALWORTHINGTON GARDENS—TEXAS

—JOE GIRON— Visually, I knew this would be a great assignment as Dime's "hut" (as he liked to call it) was a virtual carnival funhouse. The décor was New Year's Eve, 4th of July, Halloween, and Christmas all rolled up into one.

Dime's pride and joy was his 4-track room, where he wrote and recorded numerous songs. Many of the tracks were just fun songs, mocking situations or people he had observed over the course of everyday life. Other times, he would generate riffs and song ideas for future Pantera songs. It was only on the road that we would get to hear his 4-track tapes—often late at night in the midst of some drunken revelry on the bus—and they were always a source of endless amusement and laughter.

Dime was also passionate about gambling, VW Bugs, KISS, and Texas, and he decorated his house accordingly [Photo Index 30].

1997 →

The summer of 1997 saw Pantera on the bill for that year's Ozzfest. Black Sabbath had reunited to headline the tour. This was a great opportunity for Pantera to be exposed not only to hardcore metal fans, but also to the more classic rock type Sabbath fans who weren't necessarily into heavier, thrashier bands. Pantera was listed as "Special Guest" on the bill, until Marilyn Manson joined the tour halfway into the cycle. The strength of the lineup for the event ensured that Pantera would play to over 20,000 people every night.

—JOE GIRON—

EAST RUTHERFORD–NEW JERSEY

1998
2001

REINVENTING THE STEEL

—JOE GIRON—

In the second half of 1998, the band was in the process of writing the *Reinventing the Steel* album. Even though they had just released *Official Live: 101 Proof* in 1997, they were eager to work up material for this new album.

Towards the end of the year, however, an opportunity arose that was too good to pass up and their ambitions for the new album were delayed. They were asked to support Black Sabbath for a tour of US arenas that would commence on New Year's Eve 1998 and last until the spring of 1999.

I joined the band for few days during pre-production in Phoenix, the site of the New Year's Eve show. We hung out, played golf at a special Black Sabbath "Hostile Takeover" of the Raven Golf Club, and did a few new portrait shoots with the band. The shows I saw in Phoenix, Las Vegas, and Los Angeles were spectacular and watching Black Sabbath perform each night was a special bonus.

After the tour, the band returned to Arlington to write and record *Reinventing the Steel* at Dime's studio complex. The album would be released in March of 2000. You can hear Black Sabbath's influence on the album, no doubt the result of having toured together so extensively.

I was slated by the record company to fly to New Orleans to photograph the band for the album's packaging. Literally a day or two before the shoot, I was informed by the band's management that Phil wanted to use a local photographer who was a friend of his for the shoot and they no longer required my services. Needless to say, I was extremely disappointed, not just at having lost the gig, but also that Vinnie Paul, Dime, and Rex had not stood up to Phil and vetoed his decision.

There had been fractures between the Abbott brothers and Phil in the past, and these long-simmering internal tensions led to a growing rift that would divide the band into separate camps. Ultimately, this internal friction would destroy the once tightknit group of musicians who had created some of the most powerful, inspiring music at the start of the new millennium. This was the beginning of the end for Pantera.

2001 →

Pantera's official last show was on August 26, 2001 in Yokohama, Japan.

—JOE GIRON—

Their last US show was at the Tacoma Dome in Washington State and I had the good fortune to be there. I had been on assignment for a German magazine in Vancouver, BC and from there was driving down to Seattle where I would be working on a story about Pearl Jam. It just so happened that the Extreme Steel Tour would be coming to Tacoma during that same window.

I drove down to Tacoma, hung out with the band, did some work and then hung out again after the show. I took the photo of Dimebag and Kerry King of Slayer raising their Black Tooth Grin shot glasses in the air at that show. I had no idea this would be the last time I would see the band play together.

Pantera played only five more shows after that, four in Canada and their final show in Japan.

The band was in Dublin, Ireland, getting ready to begin a tour of Europe with Slayer, when the September 11 terrorist attack took place. Due to concerns for the safety of an American band touring in Europe, they took themselves off the tour.

And that's how it would end, with the band flying back to America and the four core members going their separate ways. In their heart of hearts, I assume they all thought, give it a few months and we'll hit the road again or start working a new album. But the rift between Anselmo and the Abbott brothers had grown so deep by that point that the months stretched into years with no communication between them.

New bands were formed and record contracts signed, signaling the end of the road for Pantera.

TACOMA—WASHINGTON

2001 — LONG BEACH–CALIFORNIA

—JOE GIRON— Way back in their club circuit days, Slayer's Kerry King would sometimes make it out to Texas to jam with the guys at Joe's Garage in Fort Worth. Though there was mutual admiration between the two bands, they had never toured together. That is, until the idea was formulated for the two heavyweight beasts to join forces out on the road.

—REX BROWN— These shots are from the Extreme Steel Tour when we hooked up with Slayer. Of all the bands that took us under their wing and gave a shit, Slayer was the first. They really helped us back in the day. Kerry King came down and helped us out on a few things. He just took an interest in what we were doing and helped us become what Pantera ultimately became.

As well as we knew them, we knew that they were a band you never wanted to follow live. Every night we were going up against the absolute best. It really stepped up our game and brought the band back together at a time when we really needed it. Years of touring had taken its toll, but every night we took the stage after Slayer we had to take our playing up another notch.

We didn't know this would be the last time the four of us would play together, but it was probably the tightest we had ever played and it was the epitome of what the band was all about. We had gone through everything, and after recording Reinventing the Steel, as far as heaviness, we probably didn't know where else to go. We knew at some point we needed to take a break. We had come full circle. You can see in our eyes, there was a lot of love. That tour really brought the four of us back together. We were tougher and stronger than ever before. It was the same feeling we had when we got our major label deal. All that hard work finally paying off. After everything we'd been through together, all the highs and lows, we were at our peak. The Extreme Steel Tour brought back the old feeling, but then 9-11 happened and things just stopped.

2001 PHOENIX–ARIZONA

CINCINNATI–OHIO

←2000

—JOE GIRON— This photo was taken in the summer of 2000 at Riverbend Music Center in Cincinnati, OH, before the band's set at Ozzfest. I shot other portraits on subsequent tours in 2001 of the whole band together, but this one has special meaning for me as it was the last time Phil and Dime, two highly talented, headstrong individuals, were photographed together by me.

1 — NOTES

—DEDICATION—

This book is dedicated to the memory of my grandmother, Siria Garcia Giron, my grandfather, Ralph Reyes Giron, and my mom, Frances Giron Sanchez. Without your support and encouragement, I would not have had the opportunities or vision to pursue my goal of becoming a photojournalist and music photographer. Your love and hard work helped pave the road to my dreams.

—ACKNOWLEDGEMENTS—

Thank you to my wife, Sandra Giron, for your love and support all these years.
Thank you to my publisher, Jacob Hoye, for believing in this project and not letting go of it through thick and thin.
Thanks to my editor, Gabriel Kuo.
Thanks to my photo editor, Walter Einenkel.
Thanks to Jim deBarros for bringing Jacob and I together back at MTV.
Thanks to Pantera's manager, Kimberly Zide Davis, for being open to this project from the get-go and for all the help and support provided to me over the years. I am truly grateful.
Thanks to the Pantera "Ringing Like Hell" Road Crew: Guy "Boot to the Kool" Sykes, Daryl "Bobby Tongs" Arnberger, Grady "Grand Dragon" Champion, John "The Kat" Brooks, Aaron "Wires" Barnes, Sonny "Lightning Bringer" Satterfield, "Big" Val Bichekas, Sterling Winfield & John Graham. I'm glad we all survived the traveling, rock & roll circus. And last, but not least, thanks to each member of Pantera. You gave me the opportunity to be a part of your family by opening up your lives and allowing me to capture your public and personal moments over the years. For that, "The Fifth Member" is eternally grateful.

—CREDITS—

Editor: Gabriel Kuo
Executive Producer: Jacob Hoye
Art Direction & Book Design: BRM
Text Edit: Wenonah Hoye
Photo Coordinator: Walter Einenkel
Thanks to: Roger Coletti for Vinnie Paul Abbott transcripts

—COPYRIGHT—

Copyright © 2016 Joe Giron
All Rights Reserved.

FIRST PUBLISHED IN THE UNITED STATES OF AMERICA IN 2016 BY:

LESSER GODS

Lesser Gods 15 West 36th Street, 8FL, New York, NY 10018, an imprint of Overamstel Publishers, Inc.
PHONE (646) 850-4201 / www.lessergodsbooks.com

All rights reserved. No part of this publication may be reproduced, stored in a retrieval system, or transmitted in any form or by means, electronic, mechanical, photocopying, or otherwise, without prior consent of the publisher.

DISTRIBUTED BY: Consortium Book Sales & Distribution 34 13th Ave NE #101, Minneapolis, MN 55413
PHONE (800) 283-3572 / www.cbsd.com

SECOND PRINTING: October 2016 / 10 9 8 7 6 5 4 3 2

PRINTED AND BOUND IN SINGAPORE

ISBN: 978-1944713003
LIBRARY OF CONGRESS CONTROL NUMBER: 2016939179

PHOTO INDEX

ARLINGTON TEXAS 1985

01

SUPPLEMENTAL

FORT WORTH TEXAS 1985	02	ARLINGTON TEXAS 1987	05
FORT WORTH TEXAS 1985	03	SHREVEPORT LOUISIANA 1985	06
ARLINGTON TEXAS 1985	04	DALLAS TEXAS 1985	07

INDEX

HOLLYWOOD CALIFORNIA 1991	08	OSAKA JAPAN 1992	11
LOS ANGELES CALIFORNIA 1990	09	SAO PAULO BRAZIL 1993	12
LOS ANGELES CALIFORNIA 1992	10	MOSCOW RUSSIA 1991	13

SUPPLEMENTAL

MOSCOW RUSSIA 1991	14	MOSCOW RUSSIA 1991	17
GOLD COAST AUSTRALIA 1994	15	PELHAM ALABAMA 1996	18
MOSCOW RUSSIA 1991	16	CLEVELAND OHIO 1993	19

INDEX →

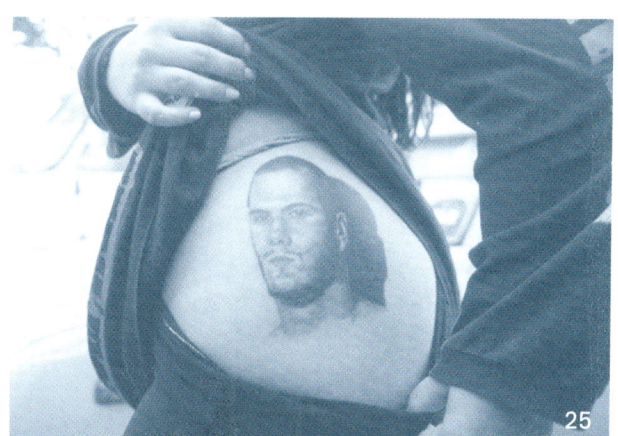

MOSCOW RUSSIA 1991	20
TOKYO JAPAN 1992	21
MOSCOW RUSSIA 1991	22

LOUISVILLE KENTUCKY 1996	23
BALTIMORE MARYLAND 1991	24
NEWCASTLE AUSTRALIA 1994	25

SUPPLEMENTAL INDEX

SAO PAULO BRAZIL 1993	26	BRISBANE AUSTRALIA 1994	29
NEW YORK NEW YORK 1994	27	DALWORTHINGTON GARDENS TEXAS 2000	30
LOS ANGELES CALIFORNIA 1994	28	SAO PAULO BRAZIL 1993	31

TOUR INDEX

COWBOYS FROM HELL

TOUR DATES
JULY 21 1990 → MARCH 31 1991

SHOWS	134
CITIES	130
COUNTRIES	19

COWBOYS & IDIOTS

TOUR DATES
APRIL 8 1991 → DECEMBER 31 1991

SHOWS	39
CITIES	36
COUNTRIES	1

VULGAR DISPLAY OF POWER

TOUR DATES
JANUARY 9 1992 → DECEMBER 14 1993

SHOWS	193
CITIES	183
COUNTRIES	20

← SUPPLEMENTAL INDEX

FAR BEYOND TOURING THE WORLD

TOUR DATES
MARCH 15 1994 ➔ DECEMBER 31 1995

SHOWS	135
CITIES	128
COUNTRIES	9

FAR BEYOND VULGAR: EUROPE

TOUR DATES
SEPTEMBER 7 1994 ➔ OCTOBER 22 1994

SHOWS	33
CITIES	33
COUNTRIES	14

WAR OF THE GARGANTUAS

TOUR DATES
JUNE 28 1996 ➔ AUGUST 26 1996

SHOWS	42
CITIES	41
COUNTRIES	1

↳ SUPPLEMENTAL INDEX

THE GREAT SOUTHERN TRENDKILL

TOUR DATES
SEPTEMBER 8 1996 ➔ DECEMBER 7 1997

SHOWS	98
CITIES	88
COUNTRIES	6

TRENDKILL AUSTRALASIAN

TOUR DATES
SEPTEMBER 10 1996  OCTOBER 1 1996

SHOWS	13
CITIES	12
COUNTRIES	3

OZZFEST 1997

TOUR DATES
MAY 24 1997 JUNE 29 1997

SHOWS	22
CITIES	22
COUNTRIES	1

WINTER TOUR 1998

TOUR DATES
JANUARY 14 1998 → FEBRUARY 5 1998

SHOWS	18
CITIES	18
COUNTRIES	1

SOUTH AMERICA 1998

TOUR DATES
MAY 6 1998 → MAY 9 1998

SHOWS	3
CITIES	2
COUNTRIES	2

← SUPPLEMENTAL INDEX

EUROPEAN TOUR 1998

TOUR DATES
MAY 30 1998  JUNE 30 1998

SHOWS	17
CITIES	16
COUNTRIES	11

WORLD DOMINATION

TOUR DATES
DECEMBER 31 1998 FEBRUARY 19 1999

SHOWS	23
CITIES	21
COUNTRIES	1

REINVENTING THE STEEL

TOUR DATES
APRIL 17 2000 ➜ MAY 20 2001

SHOWS	39
CITIES	38
COUNTRIES	17

OZZFEST 2000

TOUR DATES
JULY 2 2000 ➜ MAY 20 2001

SHOWS	29
CITIES	28
COUNTRIES	1

THE REAL STEEL TOUR

TOUR DATES
FEBRUARY 1 2001 ➔ APRIL 2 2001

SHOWS	44
CITIES	42
COUNTRIES	1

EXTREME STEEL TOUR

TOUR DATES
JUNE 20 2001 ➔ AUGUST 1 2001

SHOWS	28
CITIES	28
COUNTRIES	1

JOE & DIME
1996 ➔ ARLINGTON–TEXAS

Joe Giron's professional career began in 1983 as a staff photographer for the *Fort Worth Star-Telegram* in Texas. A chance assignment to shoot an up-and-coming local band led to a lasting friendship with one of hard rock's most revered bands, Pantera. That, in turn, led to shooting many other artists, including Nirvana, AC/DC, David Bowie, Gwen Stefani, Van Halen, and U2, just to name a handful, for many of the world's leading rock magazines. Today, his niche is in the gaming industry as the photographer for the World Poker Tour and the World Series of Poker, where he leads the photography team. He lives in Las Vegas.

Rex Brown was born in 1964 in Graham, Texas. He joined Pantera in 1982 and has also played with Down. His new band, Kill Devil Hill, is climbing the charts. He is the author of *Official Truth, 101 Proof: The Inside Story of Pantera*. He lives in New Mexico.